EXHIBITIONIST

MOLLY CROSS-BLANCHARD

COACH HOUSE BOOKS, TORONTO

first edition

Published with the generous assistance of the Canada Council for the Arts and the Ontario Arts Council. Coach House Books also acknowledges the support of the Government of Canada through the Canada Book Fund and the Government of Ontario through the Ontario Book Publishing Tax Credit.

LIBRARY AND ARCHIVES CANADA CATALOGUING IN PUBLICATION

Title: Exhibitionist / Molly Cross-Blanchard.
Names: Cross-Blanchard, Molly, author.
Description: Poems.
Identifiers: Canadiana (print) 20210156449 | Canadiana (ebook) 20210156503 | ISBN 9781552454220 (softcover) | ISBN 9781770566729 (EPUB) | ISBN 9781770566736 (PDF)
Classification: LCC PS8605.R67535 E94 2021 | DDC C811/.6—dc23

Exhibitionist is available as an ebook: ISBN 978 1 77056 672 9 (EPUB); ISBN 978 1 77076 673 6 (PDF)

Purchase of the print version of this book entitles you to a free digital copy. To claim your ebook of this title, please email sales@chbooks.com with proof of purchase. (Coach House Books reserves the right to terminate the free digital download offer at any time.)

For the young people who feel so embarrassed, all the time.

TABLE OF CONTENTS

EXHIBITIONIST

The most orgasms I ever had in one go
come over Christmas vacation
in my childhood basement bedroom:

door cracked open, sheets
peeled back, pussy
in plain view of the cat

clawing carpet. Is this how flashers feel
in their trench coats and
chest hair? I'd like to sit

in the park with my thumb stuck
up my nose and wait
for someone to notice. I want to be more

like the woman in Burger King
who eats fries straight off the floor,
the woman who cries in Walmart

when her preteen son says *Fuck you, Mom*
for the first time in front of the greeter
yanking carts. At the strip club

I eat onion rings, watch the dancer
watching me from upside down
in her halo of light. When will my roommate notice

the way I air-dry underwear on the corner
of the hallway mirror, symbol of sex
in his reflection? I want to feel

like a display-model lipstick — dug-at nub
smeared across the mouths of strangers, a much-handled
sample of the real thing.

MEET-CUTE

MEET-CUTE

I ooze honey
from my tongue
into a tiny bowl
made of chocolate
and set it in the sun
to warm

is how a poet might say *I love you*, but I
just want to say I like the way you waved
to that kid at the park and asked permission

to hold my hand. A poet might be embarrassed to tell you
they drove six hours off their route back home
for your three-hour date, or that they sobbed

as they drove away, or how when you held them
in the community garden with your eyes on their face,
time and space became real things
they cared to ignore.

If I were a poet, I might be embarrassed to tell you
I jerked off that night thinking about your hands, between my
cousin's PAW Patrol sheets. Because what
kind of freak does that?

before we've fucked in a Super 8 lounge bathroom
as Justin Investment Banker and Caroline Cocktail Waitress
pretending to have just met

on our tenth wedding anniversary, sitter at home
watching babies and HGTV. Not before handies
in a tent on top of a frosty mountain peak. I need

to grow so sick of you the grandkids say
Do they even like each other? So promise me

you'll spring for that cab, get a prostate exam,
walk away from the next dickhead with a pocket knife
who calls you *pussy*. Please

remember: rinsing raw chicken with warm water helps
the salmonella thrive, and I won't survive
not knowing how this ends.

DEAR DOLPHIN

The shaman at Broadway and Main
with a plastic shaker and some sage
says you're my *power animal*. Says
we both have big brains, like to chatter.

I don't know anything about dolphins, except
blowholes.

On the website appointment form, I wrote
Please help me like myself. Or maybe just lose
some weight.

When she put me under, I had lots of visions
of beavers, so forgive me if I don't warm up to you
right away.

I wasn't raised near the coast, hey? Far
from it.

The shaman says there's tons of food
where you're from. Squids and stuff. Says you can teach me
to just keep driving past KFC, there's rice at home.

Dolphin, I drank the mystery tincture
and laid a bundle of pink sweet pea on Wreck Beach
to be swept up and floated out to you — an offering
for your dolphin dining table
in exchange for self-discipline. To not be
such a whale? Ba-dump chh!

WE'VE ALL GOT A POEM CALLED BLOOD QUANTUM

Lying in bed you tell me we're attracted
to the genes we want and yeesh do I

ever want yours. They say it's colonial to measure your blood but
I don't wanna have to tell my babies *You're Métis, but*

Can*da says you can't have the card. Creator gave you those
good Métis cheekbones for my babies to inherit and for me

to smooch on, thick dark hair, and toe-thumbs. I've got
thyroid disease, adult acne, a high probability

of birthing twins. Like Ms. Frizzle inside Ralphie, I want to float
through your veins on a red blood cell raft, unpack my

boxes inside the curve of your aorta, sticky tack
a Buffy poster to an arterial wall. I want to duplicate myself

four times, send my bodies to the tips of each of your limbs,
and me behind your eyes. I want to see you

seeing me, the traits you'll look for
through incubator glass. Honey, I'm ready to hatch

all your toe-thumbed kin. Teach them how to walk
on their hands, wave thank you to Creator with their feet.

IT'S CLOCKWORK

how he kisses me
goodbye after a dinner
of dry chicken or fish
and some greens
cooked by me.
The way I watch him
from the third-floor window
walk to his car and leave
for the night shift
at Whiskey Dix. Wait
fifteen minutes to be sure
he's not coming back
for a forgotten wallet
or earpiece. Slip
sweats over pyjama shorts,
slink to 7-Eleven,
slide the cashier a tenner
for a box of KD
and two caramel Klondikes. Say
My nephews love this junk.
Bury the box and wrappers
under tampon applicators
in the bathroom trash, bristle-brush
neon cheese from my teeth.
How he climbs
into bed around three, rolls
onto me and I hope
for one sleepy moment
he can taste the ceremony
still on my tongue.

HOW DO YOU SUFFER?

on a snowless hill, fifty metres above the Pacific?

in eighty-dollar rain pants and a North Face jacket?

with a Fjällräven full of childhood trauma, under cover
    of the bus shelter?

walking backwards through Thunderbird Fields at midnight
    (pretending it's the prairie?)
    spotlight full blast
    (pretending it's the sun?)?

at Kabro Salon, for the sake of touch and the pressure
    of that black porcelain sink on your spine?

lost in the forest of Netflix suggestions starring Kristen Bell
    or some other white lady?

sleeping, but not dreaming
    of anything worth crying about?

always gasping awake to some sharp sound?

with permission from the new peer group?

through a pucker-mouthed smirk and wool?

in a cupboard full to the top with plastic grocery bags inside
    plastic grocery bags inside plastic grocery bags?

far too carefully? or with reckless abandon and kisses
blown east out the bedroom window?

Look at the wide sky. Now look at me. Are you ashamed to be seen
with a woman in pigtails? My tits are trapped under spandex today

because last night I pressed my bare ass against your back
and you slept on and on. Then a ghost baby with all your hair hovered
there between us, so I sang the saddest songs I knew 'til it fell
off the edge of the bed and tumbled out the open window into traffic.

I feel impotent, you say over dinner
while I cry discreetly into the scallops.
I want to tell you I don't love you
either, but you did it first so that makes me *spurned*.

Is this romance? Brine
and embarrassment, your thumb back and forth
on my wrist? Shit. I'm sorry

I wore my hair like this. You have to keep looking up
at a woman in pigtails who you don't love and that's no fun.
Should I go? Ask the sky to swallow me whole, we'll pretend
this never happened. It's cool. I never wanted a body

without your baby in it. I never wanted a baby
without your body next to mine.

JUST A SWEET SWEET FANTASY, BABY

In this one we're sitting on a quilt in the grass. He feeds
the baby a piece of mango. I wipe its chin on my shirt.

In another he helps my father fix a dishwasher, holds the tools
and acts confused when Dad forgets to plug it back in.

We don't text, only make love. When a phone rings he knows
it's not me.

We've just returned from our Tahitian honeymoon.
He puts my airplane clothes in the wash while I sleep,
sings the baby 'Dreamlover.'

A real alarm clock with hands and silver bells wakes us at six
for mushrooms, meditation, and oral.

He doesn't care that my vagina tore to my asshole and my belly
looks like sourdough starter.

I've picked a fight so he tosses me over one wide shoulder,
drops me on the bed, and buries his face in my chest, sighs
You're killing me.

He hasn't fucked the girl from work. We've fallen in love and no one else
has been allowed in. Mariah Carey shows up in that cropped hoodie
and he shuts the door on her beautiful face.

The moon is at half its orbit around earth,
he texts me for the first time since we decided not to talk.
Should look nice if you turn to the west.

I've never seen a real wheel of cheese up close
but I've seen the moon and this morning it's mouldy.
I think he meant to be romantic.

I want to tell him
about the kid I saw yesterday on the bus with an orange sucker
stuck in her hair, plastic stick pointed at the sky.

But I'm so pissed
I could crush a rock between my thumb and pointer.
I could crush his puny moon like a Cheeto.

He is the moon
at half its orbit around my five-year plan, stuck
like a sucker in my hair.

If relationships were cheese
ours would be the kind the stock boy moves
to the front of the rack to sell fast. Ours
would pair well with Ritz crackers
and Minute Maid.

If relationships were rising suns, ours
should look nice if you turn to the west.

AT 5 A.M., THE LOVE

keeps me up
like the wooden dowel
half-buried in the tomato
planter. Nudges me so close
to calling you
I have to hide

the phone inside
the glass macaroni canister, inside
the pantry with the frosted
glass door. Wants me
to cry so I scrunch my eyes
but nothing comes out.

I watch TV
but the love morphs
every man's face
into your face, even
Joey Tribbiani's face,
and laughs at me laughing

at it. Reaches through
our dog, puts its paws
on my collarbone, its nose
on my chest, perks
its ears at 6 a.m. sprinklers.
Reaches through

me, draws your penis
on a Post-it and sticks it
to the window like a first
place ribbon. I never wanted
to see the tomatoes cold and frosted
like this.

YOU THINK YOU KNOW YOUR LIFE

YOU THINK YOU KNOW YOUR LIFE
after Hera Lindsay Bird, and birth control

You think you know your life
and then you're sitting alone in the theatre with popcorn

grease on your chin watching Melissa McCarthy bumbly-stumble
from flattering floral blouse

into flattering floral blouse fifty times
in ninety minutes. Alone is what you want to be

but not feel. You think you know your life and then you're crying
because on the way to your car

you see the stars for the first time since September
and they are nothing like you

remember. All your naps begin or end
with porn. You could fill a DivaCup with pus from the zits

on your cheeks and chest. You want to fill a DivaCup
with blood but your pussy's like *Hold up.* You think

you know your life and then you piss away five hours a day
half-watching *House Hunters* reruns on basic cable and chewing

polish off your nails so you can paint them again the same shade
of Crepe-Paper Pink. Your life is wiping the kitchen counter

and signing the chore sheet, and making toast
and wiping the counter and signing the chore sheet,

and making toast. Your life is *Grey's Anatomy*
when George falls heroically in front of a bus
and ends up in the ER with his surgeon friends
but they don't know it's him because his face
is so fucked up and swollen that they treat him
like anyone else and talk shit about him while
he's lying on the table open and hurt with a tube
down his throat. You think you know your life

but then you wean yourself off 21-day Marvelon
and it turns out you haven't known your life

since your mom found a picture of your labia
on your Nokia camera phone and sent you to the clinic for a scrip.

You think you know your life but it turns out the tiny white pills
were tiny white liars pressing buttons, pulling levers, saying
Pay no attention to that man behind the curtain.

To me, you are made up —
mythology, or Warner Bros.

Understand: this is why I can't believe
you swim six hundred feet from where I sleep.

Google says your dick can grab
things, like kelp, a mackerel, a dangled
human ankle.

I do what that shaman says and print
an oversaturated 8 × 10 photo
of you, Scotch-tape it to the wall
above a Hawaiian Sunrise
candle from Save-On. You look sinister,
underlit like this. It makes perfect sense.

No hard feelings, Dolphin. You were great
in that movie with young Elijah Wood.

PUNCTURE WOUNDS

I swallowed an Atlantic Ocean
amoeba once and lost so much

weight

he told me my ass fell off.
The next time I lost that much

weight

was after he said *Molls, you let yourself go*
but Double-Sports-Bra Kathy hadn't

so he was going to live

at her place for a while.
All I could stomach for months

was Cheez Whiz toast
and gin sodas

couldn't lift the moving boxes
without dropping them hard on the driveway

but damn
do I ever look sick

in the blue revenge
dress that pushes my tits

up and out like two thin-
skinned grapefruits

ready to be ruptured
by two fat thumbs.

A girl in a pink tank top holds her own shoulders
outside the frat house. Inside, someone shouts

Fuck the patriarchy! and it warms us both. I want
to be invited in for a drink. And in the morning

I want to walk myself across the quad without one shoe
or the other. What is a *quad*? I run my tongue

along the raw spot burned away
by a hot fry. I've never been so ripe

for the picking. The girl in the tank top gets kissed
by a long-haired hockey boy and I think

of you. I hope the sad on my face looks cute
to the dudes playing flip cup on the power box. I hope

they want to save me from it. I'd like to be swept off
this curb. Who lit these street lamps and why

do they love me so much?

I'M SUCH A MODERN WOMAN WHEN I BRUNCH

alone, write with green pen on a manuscript and drip coffee stains, call it *hazard of the job* to the shy bartender. So modern, jogging on a treadmill at the Richmond gym when a clip from my hometown curling rink flickers across the mounted screen. It's modern, how I chop these scallions for a stir-fry, sprinkle sesame seeds from a shaker, from Sobeys. How I buy a deluxe car wash and sing 'Material Girl,' windows caking with tri-coloured foam. Such independence! I'm so modern on a road trip when I order too much Kung Pao chicken, walk through the Holiday Inn Express barefoot to fetch it from the thin-lipped woman at the front desk. When I drape myself across four white pillows in the manner of all modern women and watch the gas station sign flicker through slits in the blinds. Modern when my small dog — head poked out and resting on the starchy duvet — kicks me in her sleep like *wake up wake up wake up*.

and I have McMuffin wrappers on my windowsill.
You have two girlfriends and I'm in the bath
plucking hairs from my nipples with my teeth. Fuck you
if that turned you on. You have two girlfriends
on my birthday. It's my birthday
and I'm eating a bloody steak
at my desk with a plastic knife, turned away from
'The One Where Rachel Finds Out.'
I found out you have two girlfriends

on my birthday. I'm twenty-five
and smelling the crotch of all my jeans.
I'm twenty-five, in a basement suite with rats
that scratch in the walls at night and a coin-op
washer-dryer I try to shove three weeks of clothes in
at a time. Instagram says your new condo building
is round, overlooks the river walk, and you've got
a chaise longue for each of your girlfriends. I've got
a slipper for each of my feet, and I swish swish
haunt this place.

I never asked you for a million dollars.
When the rent went up and the boys stopped paying
    I never asked for money, okay?
I only asked you to help me feel less
    stressed about burnt-out bulbs, hair-clogged
    pipes, the window that won't close.
I asked if you could maybe join forces, help me
    sleep a full eight without night sweats and under-eye puff.
You guys, I'm sweating.
I'm so puffy.
I understand miracles take time but time's up, okay?
Sue told me there's four of you guys.
Four!
One for each time I cried into my hands this week
    when a coworker turned their back.
One for each sad masturbation nap.
Are you fuckers playing UNO up there?
Is that why I'm watching myself
    finger an old tea set at Value Village
    from outside my body, somewhere on a rack
    between two Christmas sweater vests?
Would you rather I asked for a million dollars?
Would you rather I wanted more
    than a decent night's sleep and Instagram skin?
It's just me and the dark. I can hear the gurgle of the sink
    and this draft through the window makes me think
    you were never with me at all.

and my mind is so lazy.
If you put a puzzle in my lap
I'll wait for the Chapels of the World
to reconstruct themselves.
I get a small headache
and shrug off any poem thought
like *Ew poetry*. I tell myself
I can write The Great One whenever
I feel like it but I never
feel like it. I'm not smart enough
for the landscape of my life, these grand libraries
and desktop computers. Why do you trust me
with *matters of insurance?* I show you
with my face that I'm stupid
and you still give me enough money
to feed myself. My taste in
music is like, whatever
Abby's vibing to on Spotify.
The last book I read was one
Cara placed in my hands. I don't know
if my pants are cool until Jasmine tells me
my pants are cool. I submit
a first draft, and they take it, sure, but
I wonder if I should tell them *Hey,*
this is not a very good poem.
My mind was lazy when I wrote it
because I decided not to drink another coffee
because I might not have been able to sleep
because I guess I need a lot of sleep

these days
but I still want to be
called a poet, so yeah, honoured
to have it in your magazine,
can't wait to see it in print.

I give the world my body
and the world gives me insomnia
and meetings in pubs where I buy
my own beer. I'm only here
because my face is white
and my grandpa sells furnaces
to all of America. I keep FaceTiming my friends
so I can cry   (I didn't come up with that myself)
((everyone on Twitter is smarter than me)).

I'm the only one who thinks
I'm fat and it's ruining every day.
I don't walk my dog enough
(it's my fault she bit the Pomeranian)
I like brussels sprouts
(I'm just not eating them)
I bought some iron pills
(they're still in the plastic)
I followed all the hot fat girls on Instagram (but still
I grab handfuls of my tummy
like *fk u*).   How many more days

can I ignore the urgent email before I'm fired? How many
can I spend staring at the philodendron
before I water it? I love when someone suffers

because then I can help them.
No one is helping me through this suffering
except Mom but duh she doesn't count   (well actually

maybe they're trying to help me and I'm saying
no thank you I don't want to go for ice cream tonight).

It's been raining and raining so I slink to the window and
picture this: Mom pulls up in the Buick. I sprawl across
the back seat and leave everything behind, even the books.
On the prairie, I play *Paper Mario* in the basement for hours
while Reece feeds me the crusts from her grilled cheeses.
And when she's at school I lie on the trampoline watching
the birdfeeder I made in freshman shop class. No birds come
(but I've given the world my body and the world has given
it a rest).

WAY OUT, OR

POEM I WROTE WHILE JOGGING ON 12TH AVE

If that Purolator van hops the curb, crushes
my pelvis and spleen, New Balance tumbling acrobatic
into the intersection free of my body, triumphant
bloom of blood across my sweats. If I'm tube-fed
in the hospital and my body has to eat
its own fat while my exes watch
from the visitors' wing, distraught
and horny. I'm unable to sit upright,
my new job has to be done by someone
else. I'm released from my contract. I'm *brave*,
not depressed. Pointing to each purple scar,
the brace around my neck, the needle
pumping morphine into my wrist, I say *See? This
is why*. And the bosses say *You poor thing*.

A lawyer from the TV show *Suits* goes to court for me,
wins a giant settlement from Purolator.
I never have to work again. I heal. My body
meets this dismembering with fervour
and I'm stupid beautiful. Edward Cullen
has drained me of my mortal blood
and filled my flesh with liquid marble.
While the sexy physical therapist is testing
the mobility of my new titanium hip, he can't help
himself, he eats my pussy and then
tells me I taste like peaches and I really do
taste like peaches. When we swap
tender vows 'til death do us, two doves
fly a heart around the sun.

the fatphobia
in that last poem, and others.

Most days, I put a piece of cloth on my body and it feels like
pushing pretzel rods lengthwise down my throat.
I'm the best person I've ever known but still I cry an hour

before the beach picnic. I fantasize about not being
in this body anymore and I write poems about those fantasies.
Then someone offers to publish the poems,
which people might read.

People might read the poems
and then flip to the author photo
and they could think *Yes, fat*
but more likely *Yeah, right.*
When it's just me and a mirror, I can't tell if I'm *yesfat* or *yeahright*

which is a privilege and also a mean trick
by the fashion industry, which calls me
Mid-size (adj): a person who is between size 10 and 16
who can usually find a floral dress off the rack at Urban Outfitters
which fits too loose and too tight and is completely useless and
who has googled 'body dysmorphia' once a week since she was twenty.

I don't know how to write this poem but to not write this poem
would be cowardly. So I hope you'll understand when I say
I sometimes hate my body but I don't hate fat bodies.
I sometimes fear the fat on my body and I resent the feeling.

I resent the mother, and the mother's mother, and the
mother's mother's mother who said *Yay!*
when the Christmas clothes fit but it felt like *Congratulations*

to your body, and mostly I resent the world that made the mothers
fear their babies' bodies and their own, skip chocolate pie
and the family photo. Mom, I'm sorry we don't love our whole
selves. I'm sorry we're such cool fucking people poisoning our minds
every day with our minds. In an interview someday, someone
might ask *Did you ever cry writing these poems?* And I'll say
Just one. And they'll say *Which one?* And I'll say
The one where my mother gets hurt, too.

If I shave my head I'll learn
who my real friends are. I look and look

at my eyebrows but never know for sure
where to pluck. I tell my reflection *Don't worry,*
your blue lipstick is cute. I tell her
I love you and we don't know why

we're crying. At the gym, to be brave,
I walk slowly
to the showers
in my new red thong.
Next week I will even look
straight at the mirror
like Arcimboldo
at a gourd. I eat a bit

of mould and call it immunization. Brush
my dog's back teeth for ten seconds and call it
'Accomplishment' on my cv. When I fill
an online shopping cart I delete everything

except the best yellow sweater, wear it
for three sleeps, and am so happy
for a time.

I'M A WOMAN WITHOUT A LOVER

so I dutch-oven my dog on the daily
masturbate to Zac Efron in the propaganda film *The Lucky One*
take a lot of walks to the store for herbs and limes
talk to the ceiling at night like *absolve me of this agony*
freeze Crock-Pot meals
play the drums on my pussy mound to the beat of 'Hakuna Matata'
don't wonder if I'm pretty
don't even want a shitty boyfriend to carry my tote
      through the conservatory
carry my own tote
touch a prickly pear
suck the bead of blood 'til it clots
grit is a thing we have in common, amiright, ladies?
masturbate to Taylor Schilling in the propaganda film *The Lucky One*
throw out Crock-Pot meals and call it KonMari
idle in the Safeway parking lot sipping peppermint mocha
      to Ariana's Christmas album like *shit that's good*
talk to my thyroid like *why u such a lazy bitch*
watch the days keep coming like *get comfy, girl*
set the scene like I'm the main character in a movie about
      a heartbroken poet living in the big city with her typewriter
      and a Chiweenie, who stirs orange bitters into a cocktail
      with a pencil then tucks it behind her ear
      when — gasp! — Zac Efron enters the saloon in a fringe jacket
      and swaggers over like *how are you single, little miss*
watch the credits roll and think about the next time I'll be kissed

ARE YOU THERE MOLLY? IT'S ME, HYMEN.

[shwoop!]

[applause]

[heavy breathing]

I'm as surprised as you are.

Last thing I remember, we were fifteen
and you'd just sucked your first dick.
I was so proud of you.

Molly, what happened?
I thought I was dead.

I thought … Well, ifI'mbeinghonestIthoughtyoukilledme.

[cricketcricket]

Anyways.

You've grown up. Cool tats.

The place is just like I left it. Thanks for dusting
the drapes. But did you happen to come across
my *One Tree Hill* Season Two DVD box set?

[rummaging]

Never mind, found it!

Let's catch up over Canesten and Lemisol.

Molly, you're not very chatty.

Should we masturbate with the minty Mr. Sketch marker?
That always cheered you up.

What do I have to do, buy a longboard
and quote *Infinite Jest*?

Autonomous regeneration isn't easy, you know.
The least you could do is talk to me.

Maybe I should have just stayed dead then, huh?

Okay. That's it. I'm going.
You'll NEVER have to DEAL with me AGAIN.

[grunting]

[straining]

[panting]

Um. Molly?

Okay, so I tried to go but I — I don't know how.

I think maybe there's something … you … have to do?

Like, okay. How'd you get rid of me last time?
Just do that again.

Do it now, I'm ready.

Do it.

…

Are you doing it?

WHEN WE'RE YOUNG

WHEN WE'RE YOUNG AND INSECURE ABOUT OUR
INTELLIGENCE
   after Monica McClure

Serena never talks to her mom on the phone
while she's pooping. As soon as she buys toilet paper
Serena takes it out of the plastic and puts it in a drawer.
Has she seen me flick a booger at the floor? Serena never
sticks loose hair to the wall when she showers, and she knits
while she's watching Netflix. I don't do anything
while I'm watching Netflix.

Serena has the coolest clothes. She wears these shoes
you'd only see in a Billie Eilish video. Billie Eilish
is seventeen. When I was seventeen I was so worried
about the hem of my Giant Tiger jeans. Now I read
my horoscope and itemize each sadness
in a notebook. Billie Eilish reads her horoscope
and has her people build a theme park. Serena
reads her horoscope and just can't be bothered.

One time I ran out of toilet paper and used
a torn-off piece of tampon box to wipe. When Billie Eilish
runs out of toilet paper, her people go to Walgreens
and then she makes toilet-paper cranes and crushes them
with her butt cheeks for a music video, and it's ART. Serena
never runs out of toilet paper. When Serena leaves a party
to poop, and upon her return a friend hands back her vodka soda
asking, *How was your poop?* she never
replies, *Disappointing.*

about germs. I'll eat a linty pocket mint. I'll eat dirt
just for the shock of it. In the bathroom stall
I inhale another person's period. Sometimes I go
in there just to pick my nose. An imagined audience
watches me shit so I cross my ankles to the side
like Anne Hathaway in *The Princess Diaries*
when she gets her hair straight and learns how
not to be gross. But my hair is still straight
when I touch the brownish wax on the Q-tip before
the tossing. I'm such a loud puker and I splatter
on his sneakers at the park. In eighth grade,
on a dare, I dunk my whole head in a bucket of grey water
collected from a hole in the roof of Jessi's attic.
When I come up for air and my dirty hair sops
all over my shirt, he's watching Jessi
make an absent-minded braid and I don't
even care. I don't even care.

I imagine you missed the staff meeting where they doled out extra-curriculars.

I've never used the words *vas deferens* but I say *ball sack* a lot.

You taught us about condoms. How they prevent every bad thing. In purple gel pen on a piece of loose-leaf: *Sexually Transmitted Diseases. Pregnancy. Death.*

But you didn't teach us how to get to the point of needing a condom.

You didn't teach me I wasn't sexy.

I walked into that MSN group chat unprepared for my last-place rating, Mr. Decker.

I walked into a game of Spin the Bottle not knowing it would end as soon as the mouth landed on me.

You didn't teach us that when you eat a family-sized bag of Cheese Pleesers and fart on a boy as a joke to show him how down-to-earth and funny you are, he won't want to make out with you.

He'll want to make out with the new girl from Meadow Lake instead, because her hair moves like silk and she has a tan in the winter, and she only farts in the privacy of her own home.

You took the boys to a different classroom, so I didn't learn about me whatever they learned about me.

Are you the reason they keep trying to scoop out my cervix like pumpkin guts?

In a perfect world, you would've shown us all some hardcore porn. At least then they could hurt us in a way that we'd like.

Controversial, I know. But most of us had parental blocks on our family-shared desktops. Think of the visual learners, Mr. Decker.

I'd like to tell you about the first time I had sex but I can't actually pinpoint it.

Mr. Decker, you didn't teach us about the pre-sex sex.

Where you drive the family van out to the bush and lay a towel on the backseat. Grind your parts together, and it's sticky and it hurts, but you're not sure anything broke inside you.

And while he's digging a hole for the empty condom with his hands, you think: did the thing break in second grade when you fell with a leg on either side of the monkey bars and it ached so bad you held your throbbing crotch until recess was over?

You should have taught us that *hymen* is a metaphor for *pure*, and also *prude*. Which one you are depends on what he says about you on Xbox Live.

I'd like to tell you about the second time I had sex but I was asleep.

Okay, it was more like the three thousand and second time.

Sometimes we did that. Sleep sex.

Like I'd be sleeping.

And he would start having sex.

And then we'd both be having sex.

And it was hot, I think.

You taught us that pubes were things we had, but not all the politics.

You didn't teach me how to love my pubes, Mr. Decker, so a boy taught me how to hate them.

He'd slip his hand down the front of my jeans to decide whether or not we'd have sex that night.

I'm just kidding, jeez!

Then he'd pretend to fall asleep while I locked up the house.

A story for you: the boys in Mr. Smith's second-grade class had an obsession with our *panties*. I didn't like the word *panties* to begin with.

They'd use us to get to each other, that was their shtick. The biggest boy would grab the smallest girl's elbows and pull them behind her back, while the most popular boy, the Danny Zuko of the group, would address us, her cohort. *If you don't want us to hurt her*, he'd say, *show us your panties.*

We'd shout back at him, tell him to stop being such a turd, throw pine cones and pebbles from a safe distance. But then the small girl would begin to cry. And Kenickie would laugh and hold her tighter.

I was the first to lift my skirt. One was always good enough for them. They'd let the small girl go and she'd wipe snot off her face and pretend none of it bothered her very much, and we'd all go play marbles in the shale together as if nothing out of the ordinary had happened.

You didn't teach me about ass stuff, Mr. Decker.

A boy taught me about ass stuff when we were drunk and he was feeling bold.

Bite down on something.

Then we both laughed at the half-circle mascara marks on my pillow the next morning.

Ha. Ha.

You juggled so many props — bananas, a dirty toothbrush, an overhead projector slide of a uterus like a Rorschach — that I think you forgot to talk about love.

How love would be the best and worst thing to ever happen to us.

How we'd eat nothing but saltines and ginger ale for months falling in and out of it.

Mr. Decker, you didn't teach me how to drive to Ella's house at midnight to explain to her through tears why I slept with her ex an hour before.

How to tell a prop from a soulmate.

That she'd say, *He has a way of making it seem like your idea*, would still help me move my furniture the next day, offer to buy me a breakfast crepe.

I would've liked to know that if a man is in your bed and you wish
he wasn't, you can recall all your favourite lines from *Shrek* until you
fall asleep:

That is a nice boulder.

Tripping over themselves like babes in the wo-hoods.

I'm making waffles.

What is semen made of?

You probably did teach us that, Mr. Decker, but I forget.

The best sex I ever had was on a Disney vacation.

I'd gained some weight but he didn't seem to mind that night, there on the warm Florida floor between our rented twin beds.

He felt for all the extra parts of me.

He wanted me to know I was craved.

Mr. Decker, you didn't warn us this would be fleeting.

Regrettably,
Molly

FIRST-TIME SMUDGE

It takes eight matches, a burnt thumb, and a quick Google search
to light the sweetgrass braid Mom scored for me from an elder
at work. *Always use matches*, she said. *Spirit likes matches.*

I don't have the abalone shell or eagle feather —
water and air — so I just hold them in my mind, cup the smoke
to my face, my left chest, down the fronts of my calves
to my feet. I notice too late I forgot to change the Spotify playlist
to something more traditional. Hopefully Spirit likes
Jimmy Eat World. I think about the word *smudge*

while I coax the smoke into each corner of my bedroom, the way
it might mean *a smeared mark*, like how the message from him
apologizing for the women in my bed was a smudge

on my inbox today. The way I felt when I read it, a smudging of my cool
front. I want to think of the word *smudge* as *wiping away* but
to soil is simpler than to cleanse and I'm afraid all this smoke
can't smudge his spirit from the air here. I open the window, cough

an acrid cough into the dark. I notice too late: the Google article said
to keep it open from the very beginning.

and it's been five years. Is there a best-before stamp on feeling
sorry for yourself? When heartache expires, what does it
taste like? I dream about him

four nights every month, during PMS. Tonight
he spins me in circles at the edge of a cliff and sings
a country song in my face — Luke Bryan. And I'm back

at Craven, when I got alcohol poisoning and couldn't make it
through Luke's set, so he followed three feet behind me
through the campsite even though I told him to stay. He slid into the car
with a muted martyrdom I'd only ever seen from my mother
on her birthday and cracked a window to listen from afar. In my dream

he doesn't shush me like he did that night
while I puked hard during 'Play It Again.' In my dream
I'm the girl whose tan legs are swinging.

I WANT TO CALL YOU NOW AND EVERY TIME

I drive across the prairie.

I'm asleep at the wheel of this life
drinking soup and swerving
    into oncoming traffic.

When you rubbed your face from side to side across my naked
stomach like a dog with an itch it was more sex
than all the rest put together.

I'm spilling on myself.   When I scoop out
a wonton with one hooked finger will
I remember what it is to be animal?

I remember when you pawed my bare back each time
I stretched for a drink of water in the night.
I pretended not to like it
drank so much water
    spilled on your sheets.

    Country music is shit but
I'm listening to your playlist called *Kick it in the sticks* and

I can breathe.   The road is so smooth.
I keep on spilling.

WINNIPEG, YOU'RE SO PRETTY

in the dark, monuments
lit from underneath to mask
the pocks in your marble.

You hoard Freezie sleeves and cigarette butts
in your snowbanks when you know May
will spit them into the streets
and that's a symptom of insanity.

Tell my friends I can't talk today.
I'm moving through you
with the open-coated lilt of someone
already too cold to care.
I've made a quinzee of my chair
and this cup of Lipton tea.

Let loose a little
icicle over my ex's windshield
so he knows I'm thinking of
that girl, that time, in my bed.

Winnipeg, I'm mad at you. My spine's a necklace of knots
and it must be your fault.

Do you like it when *Maclean's* calls you
on your shit? Does it make you
want to be a better city?

I bet you were smoking dope under the bleachers
when Toronto scored the game-winning goal.
You'll be my bridesmaid when I marry Vancouver.

Dr. Phil says middle children get neglected.
Do we hug you enough?

I'm sorry we keep putting Band-Aids
over your asphalt wounds. I don't blame you
for taking out my front struts.

My New Year's resolutions
are underneath the snow pile
in the Costco parking lot.
I buried them there after
exchanging a midnight kiss for weed
in your underground pub.

Winnipeg, let's get forked
under the bridge and laugh at people
who make moving through you look easy —
as if they can't see those cracks, in the ice, on the Red.

WE USED TO GO TO THIS DESSERT BAR

across the street from our apartment complex
between the dry cleaner with the little dogs on the logo
and the cafe with the good jam. The dessert bar

was called Dessert Sinsations, and each slice of cake
cost twelve dollars, so we'd stand in front of the glass
display case arguing the merits of Oreo versus mango,

chiffon versus sponge. Then we'd walk our one piece of cake
back across the street, sit in the chairs we took
from the Booster Juice where we worked as kids,

and eat it with two forks, in a quiet circle
of kitchen light. When we meet up for the first time

after years apart, it's at the cafe
with the good jam. Dessert Sinsations has closed
and I think the metaphor too obvious

to mention. We order coffees and watch each other
for changes in milk and sugar preference, move our eggs
around our plates until he sighs and says *I'm too anxious to eat*

and I'm so relieved because this is the one thing
we were good at, and if we can't do this
then it's over, it really is.

PLEASE DON'T SUE ME, MEGHAN TRAINOR. THIS IS NOT A POP SONG.

Dear future husband, sometimes I imagine you watch me
while I do some menial task, like season a cast-iron pan or vacuum
the blinds. I haven't met you yet but I really think you'd like
the wistful face I make when I de-ice the refrigerator. I think you might
admire my wherewithal, the way I don't need you at all.

Dear future husband, I thought you were the vegan bodybuilder
who took me skating but didn't know how to skate. The bouncer
with a belly like a bald kiwi fruit.

I never thought you'd be a famous person, husband,
but when Danny danced to Aaliyah on *The Mindy Project*
I hoped you could be him.

Dear future husband, I don't believe in tradition but
I'd like a long engagement, and a party. I won't take your name
or toss a bouquet, but let's rent a nacho-cheese fountain.

Dear future husband, do you watch *Teen Wolf* and wish
you looked like Tyler Posey? I do.

But if you have a scar on your face from a snow-machine accident
and your beard is patchy, and you have three curly hairs
that grow just above your butt crack, I'm sure they'll grow on me.

Dear future husband, you should know I'm kind of fucked up.
I move fast through the day to make myself smaller
for you, even though I know you're nothing like him.

Dear future husband, I've cleared a drawer in the dresser
for your T-shirts and socks. The 'shaman' called this
manifest destiny but Taylor calls it nuts. She doesn't know
how close you are, how we once rode a bus together
and you wanted to say hi but got scared, how
the next time we ride the 16 you'll raise a hand
to be seen and say, *Right here.*

I'll be so good at giving birth
and while getting pregnant the father will make me cum
three times. I won't care about the style
of my maternity jeans and the not caring

will make me so cool. I'll stop fucking with lipstick.
I will love my growing body and also my doctor will say
You're a bit on the thin side for the seventh month but
nothing to worry about. The father will rub my belly

with oil every day and I won't have one
stretch mark, not even on my ass. Especially not
on my ass. His mother will visit twice and they'll be such
nice weekends. She'll buy us coffee-table books

and I'll read them in the morning with scrambled eggs
and herbal tea from David's. I'll read in one that babies
who are a product of orgasm make more friends in school
and I'll pat the father on his head. I'll crave

carrots and hummus. When I march through Whole Foods
in slippers because of the swelling, the clerk will think me so
eccentric. I'll have a glass of wine because the doula says it's fine.
I'll be so good at giving birth that even the old nurse

who's birthed four babies herself will mutter
Tough cookie while I'm ripping. The baby will have
brown hair because blonde ones are always getting sick. The baby
will infect the poems and the resulting book will go largely

unnoticed, but oh well. I'll be one of those people
who don't leash their dog and nothing bad happens.
The dog will climb into the baby's chair for snuggles
right when a camera is on them. When a camera is on me

I'll always be laughing in that happy-humble way.

WHAT DO YOU DO?

WHAT DO YOU DO?

When you brush your teeth do you get toothpaste on the mirror or are you a cyborg?

Do you sleep naked or do you suck?

Have you ever talked to the moon as a friend?

Where did you grow up? Did it have a water park? Did the fair come through every August and did you piss yourself a little on the Ring of Fire?

Is this haircut negotiable?

Do you have roommates? Are they also blond? Do you and your roommates sit knee-to-knee on a futon drinking pale ales and watching *The Office* while someone pours queso over a plate of Tostitos?

Sorry, that was pointed.

Have you been on the apps long? Have you ever swiped left on every nice-looking person because you felt undeserving of love?

What time of day do you masturbate, mostly? Do you think about an authority figure or a lesser mortal? Am I the kind of person who could make you hard? Don't answer that.

White liquor or brown?
Fucking or friendship?
Land Back or rEcoNciLiAtiOn?

Do I intimidate you? I know you can see my areolas through my T-shirt and yes it's a power move but I really am a sweet girl, just ask my therapist from when I was twelve and too anxious to have sleepovers.

Did you go to therapy when you were twelve or does your spirit stay in your body when you talk to your birth father on the phone?

How many pets have died since you were old enough to feel that perverse loss? What were their names? Where on your body are they tattooed?

Are you going to let me live my life or are you going to sit me at a dinner table with your sexist friend Steven?

Are you going to be pissy if I write poems about how much sex we are or aren't having? And if I say, *Okay then I'll write about my other boyfriends*, will you throw a beer glass, not at my head, but not *not* at my head?

Will your mother look at me across the yard at the engagement barbecue with pity all over her face because she knows she raised a shitbag and hopes there's something I can do about it?

Should we make out?

JUNIOR CHICKEN

He feeds me a bite, starfished
on his mattress on the floor. Our ankles touch
like Lincoln Logs. *Did I make you cum?*
he asks, a glob of McChicken sauce on his chin.

It's just mayo, I say,
send my hand like a scope
into the sheets. It comes back miraculously
with my underwear. *They want you
to think it's special but it's not.*

Today, I apologized to my vagina
for all the recent shaving and latex
and whatnot. I said, *I'm sorry*
but we're back in the game now
and everyone's making sacrifices.

Today, an all-time low:
I used my sister's old kindergarten scissors —
her initials still on the blade
in permanent marker —
to trim my pubes.

Today, I used my Universal Studios Orlando mug
to heat butter for popcorn
and dropped the sack of kernels on the floor
and it was just enough to make me cry.

Today, a man brought me pizza at 2 a.m.
and then said my hair smelled nice
like his Grade 9 girlfriend
so a bit of a mixed bag, you see.

Today, my dog leaned her neck
into a squashed sandpiper carcass
and rubbed.

Today, I wanted a smoke
for the suppression
and to be choked.

Today, I read his tweets
on the toilet with the shits.

There's no such thing
as coincidence.

TO THE DRUMMER FROM HALIFAX WHO SHARED MY ICE CREAM CONE BUT DIDN'T STAY THE NIGHT

I'm crying over you like we were in love.

Didn't I ride your bike around the parking lot and didn't you take a sneaky picture of me on it?

Yeah. We were in love.

Listen: we have a mutual friend who hosts a lot of backyard potlucks and it's gonna be a problem.

The tarot cards said not to be impulsive so I've refrained from showing up and shitting in your cigarette-butt coffee can.

I think I love you because Ellie hates men but she didn't even bark when you hiked me up around your hips.

All of this is a bad movie script I can't stop writing, starring Candace Cameron Bure.

Do you look at the picture of me on your bike and wish you'd called?

Do you say, *That's one fun quirky girl I'll never get back?*

When we get married, I'll read this poem at our wedding and we'll laugh.

And while we're dancing, you'll whisper in my ear, *Thank god you didn't take a massive deuce on my front porch.*

DEAR DOLPHIN III

Good news! My wardrobe is all blue
and grey sweaters now. When I wear
the periwinkle vest, I flap my flippers

and think of you. I'm sorry you're smart
as an ape without the thumbs. I'm sorry
I thought your kin were the dumb blonds
of the sea. When you think of me

do you breach so hard
your girlfriend gets jealous? Let's play
Ariel and Prince Eric, where you're Ariel

and I'm floating by
ready to snag
any pretty wet thing
in my net, bring it home,

and watch it try to talk, drown it
in a bubble bath.

Like I said, no
hard feelings.

to have my permanent retainer removed and the receptionist who greets me wants to know why. I tell her it's hard to eat apples and popcorn, my two favourite foods. I don't tell her I want to give better blowies because once, at King's Head Pub, Caleb let slip over beers that you told everyone I made you bleed and now I have a rep for slitting frenulums like some sort of succubus. I don't tell her I'd rather be a gap-tooth bitch than a peen paper-shredder. I don't tell her that when the metal is gone my tongue will poke around all that new space 'til it touches you.

YOU

are a ghost in bed beside me.
are the smell under my fingernails hours after sex with myself.
are that UFC fight where Silva snaps his calf in half
 and they replay it fifty times over.
are every athletic impulse I'll ever have.
are über jock.
walk with me in the supermarket and put kale in my cart.
turn my jeans in on themselves, appraise the tag and sigh
 What happened?
pass out in the corner while both my hands clutch the edge
 of our washing machine.
give me permission to eat half an apple with peanut butter
 after 8 p.m.
play *cop* for Halloween. I'm *sexy prisoner.*
invade my inbox, subject *I'm sorry.*
make me write a list of things I still love about you:
 wolf teeth, warm hug, asthma laugh.
make me forgive you, for real.
belong to her now. She is making bannock with our mother.
watch me fuck our high school friend, hover above us
 in the room with the giant green water tank
 and a lava lamp.
watch me cry over you in my car, at a stop light.
bribe the seagulls with chunks of bread to check up on me,
 don't you?
are a fist-sized hole in the drywall of my heart, covered up
 by a framed painting of Iron Maiden's *Killers.* This
 is a bad metaphor but so are you.

are the baby crow fallen out of its nest downtown
     we decide too late to save. This is a good metaphor
     because it's true.
would think I'm so fat now.
wouldn't be wrong.

THIS IS A POEM I'VE FASHIONED

from a journal entry.

Sorry.

I was hysterical one night.

The moon was being weird.

I sent you nudes that made my ass look rounder than it is and wrote
I think we should have sex when I'm in town.

I put a deposit down on a hand tattoo that Kyle says will make me
look like I've been to prison.

I ate half a vegan bean wrap and a piece of cheez toast and two cups
of sweet beige coffee and that's it.

I took a pissing selfie and posted it in the ladies' fitness accountability
chat, #multitasking. No one liked it.

Is this what feeling my whole life is like?

is what I wrote in the journal.

I'd been watching *Fleabag*, that was the problem.

Phoebe Waller-Bridge, and the moon.

I reminded myself that my mother and my best friend are alive.

I reminded myself I have a dog, not a guinea pig.

She licked my hand over and over and I had to lie still for a while.

I read some Sally Rooney and just like that the banana peel drying on the desk became endearing.

I was endeared to myself, but now I can't remember how.

Recalling drunkenness, sober.

I need you to love me more than I need to remember liking myself and I'm only a little embarrassed to admit it.

I hope you like my body when we fuck.

I hope you say my asshole tastes like caramel again.
Never forgot that.

And I hope my asshole actually tastes like caramel and you weren't just saying it to make me feel better about having a regular-tasting asshole.

If you haven't missed my breasts, you will after you see them in these new sheer cups.

You'll miss them while they're still in your hands.

All of it happened so fast.

I just wanted to feel loved again by a man who loves me — to be held so normal while it's dark outside — and I wanted to smell you.

This is the present tense. ˙

I want to lick your warm neck and smell that magic thing my spit does on your skin.

Love really looks like this, huh.

This is the transition.

I'm climbing a hill or else descending quickly into a tumble.

If I'm a baby's light-up toy, you're the blinking default setting.

I have to be loving someone else to not be loving you.

What we thought was a pressed red self-destruct button is actually hundreds of windows to be nailed shut by hand.

Do you understand?

This coming together is part of the leaving.

Sorry.

Just fuck me like you did at Disney World.

I swear I'll be right there with you.

WHOEVER INVENTED CRUISE CONTROL JUST WANTED TO FUCK THEMSELF

on a prairie highway. The experience is lukewarm at best —
you can't be the fastest car on the road and also have
the most explosive orgasm. But now I've done it

and that makes me cooler than you. I rinse my pussy fingers
in the last sip of gas station coffee at the bottom
of the styrofoam cup. I love to share

a secret with myself. Here's a secret I keep telling my friends like
an excuse: my body forgot how to make an orgasm
with another person. I look like a woman

who doesn't have a lot of sex, but I want everyone to know I like
a finger in my ass and I'll stick one in
yours. Will I ever cum again

out of the driver's seat? This is on-the-nose but sometimes
you just can't fuck around. It's cool to masturbate
in a moving car. It's not cool

to fuck your ex, and instead of stealing all his clothes and locking
him outdoors to be humiliated, you ask him
to stay the night. The worst thing

is to know you're too good for someone you want. The worst
betrayal is the one you do to yourself when you tell him
I'll always love you. Here's a secret

you should know: I've always been an earnest bitch. I've always loved this way — foot off the pedal and coasting, coasting.

get drunk and tell your dad about your lover on the coast, how he
asked for cling wrap to pack up the pizza for next day's lunch, left

you with hickies and your sheets in the tub. Eat cookie dough
unbaked by your mother with love. Lie on the dirty carpet

and hold their rez dog against your chest 'til she bites
your face. Let her crush you. Take your breath away. Kiss your sister

on the head too long to be okay. Decorate that tree,
baby. Cry over Baby's 1st Xmas 1993. Eat so much shredded cheese,

go back for more. Watch *Jurassic Park* and call it Christmas
spirit. Watch *A Christmas Story* and cry out of fear of that red-headed

fuck, Farkus. Scream, *We should have known Morgan Freeman was
a dumbass when he guest-starred in Ted 2!!!* So many

soap commercials on TV. So much pressure to be clean. It's 22 below.
Sit on the front step and let the snow pile up on your head. Hold that

feeling for later. Of being buried on the prairie. Post a titty pic
on Tinder. Ignore dick from high school

in your DMs. Say to the vegan muffins from the band concert
bake sale, *I'm sorry you're not who I hoped you'd be.*

PINKY DRUM
after Rosanna Deerchild

Hey babe, it's Mom. I know you're asleep but I just woke up from a dream and I think it might make a good poem. I don't know if this is how poems work but I figure I'll tell you anyway.

There was a drum in my pinky. Like a powwow drum. Just this little beat that grew bigger and louder through the day. I kept asking my friends to listen but they couldn't hear it.

I guess I must be feeling bad for telling you the other day that you've only got about a pinky's worth of Métis in you. That was a shitty thing to say. I know that's not how it works.

That's how I feel about being Métis, hey? Like it's this little drum beating just for me. And it doesn't really matter that no one can hear because I know it's there. You know it's there, right?

Anyways. I'll try you again in the morning. Love you. Bye.

PUT IT ON MY TOMBSTONE:
'IT WAS JUST HER PERSONALITY'
with found material from an episode of Seek Treatment *podcast*

I try so hard. Desire is colonized and I am
winning. I link to Instagram. I post my face
and list my race. It looks so different depending
on the angle. My personality is that I've been broken
up with. I just need to be validated through sex. I don't feel

hot today. The dermatologist got in my head. I'm a liar
when I eat a salad and go *mmm*. When someone says abs are made
in the kitchen I tell them to seek treatment. But I would
rather not have sex than have sex with someone
who's not hot. I never wanted to be this

person. You've just asked a question and I'm already
blank. Look at me. I want you to get hard and treat me
with care. I'm fragile. I'm bad at opening doors
with keys. This will send shockwaves through
the community: I've never done something I loved.

Once upon a time we met through mutuals.
    His shirts were just normal shirts and wow that's rare.
    We went for lunch and I thought *tall.*
    We did a stupid hug with my foot off the curb.

Twenty-six dates later and there are affirmative words like
    missed you and *good at sex.*
    Eating lasagna then fucking to the sounds
    of a flat-earth documentary.
    Skin-care bundle for my birthday.
    Leather toiletries bag for his.

He made me cum once and damn what a trick.
    Ask Google: This mean love?
    Tired clit say: No honey.
    Ask Google: How to know when love?
    Clit say: When all he gotta do is touch your hand.

Accidental boyf touches my hand and it's like
    okay Paul from the *Gilmore Girls* revival.
    It's like why am I here I want to be home
    farting under my own covers.

I know he wouldn't mind my farts, he's a good man.
    He'd stand in the kitchen with me
    scooping strawberry cream cheese with Triscuits.
    He'd look at my car like
    ah here's the problem.

He's not like the others :) but he's not like the others :(
    When he kisses me with tongue at the back door
    I wish I felt *Okay I can stay* and not
    Going to Arby's without u.
    I wish I wish.

A good man wants to be my boyf so I go with it because
    I deserve a good man, you see?
    I'm not fucked up at all, look
    at these healthy behaviours.
    Look how he kisses my nose and remembers
    the stories I tell him and look at me
    not running from that stuff. Standing so still
    you'd think there's no place I'd rather be.

BUT IF

I abandoned my life to live on a boat.

the boat could drive itself.

I picked you up at a port in Regina.

we sailed in circles on the prairie like kind pirates.

we went below deck and made a baby.

you braided and unbraided my hair every day.

the apocalypse came when we were under a tarp
with our dicks out.

the people we loved most were bobbing by and we scooped
them up in a big net.

they each possessed a necessary skill for survival.

we learned to like the taste of raw pike.

I was so happy I never questioned it.

money was a thing you stuffed the pillows with.

you held me each night while the big flood rocked us to sleep.

our baby was between us with their eyes open and their hands on our faces.

our baby took care of us in our old age.

our baby got old.

we died and came back as beavers.

we built a home for our old baby and they built a fire in it
while we watched from the bank across the strait holding paws.

while we were holding paws, you tickled my palm
with one dull claw and said, *This was the plan all along.*

because it's a book written by a woman
and it checks the woman's book vibes:
Heartbreak? Check.
Ghost children? Check.
Yearning? Checkeroony, baby.

When they call this *a vulnerable exploration of womanhood*
will they cite the ass stuff or say
she was hurt so good? Is it vulnerable
to write *I love my massive rack* or is it
just a fact? I want to tell you

everything — like how I fantasize
about lifting a car off all four sisters, pulling Dad from
a burning barn, jumping off a bridge
to save a Jack Russell Terrier — but then
I'd have to divorce myself

from myself. Vulnerability is tricky
like that. *Fake it 'til you make it,*
Mom always says, and here's
the book. Susan asked: *Can the last poem
be just about you?* and it's a trick question because

it's always been about me. When
I'm staring into your face and it's like
you're the only man I've ever loved
I'm really thinking about the next time
I'll feel so alive.

ACKNOWLEDGEMENTS

As an uninvited guest on the West Coast, I would like to acknowledge that this collection was written on the traditional, unceded, and ancestral territories of the xʷməθkʷəy̓əm, Səl̓ílwətaʔ, and Skwxwú7mesh peoples. This land held me with care while I sifted through some pretty major bullshit, and I will be forever thankful for it and its protectors.

'But if' and 'Granville Island' were published in *The Malahat Review*. Thanks to editor Iain Higgins.

'Pinky drum' was published in *Red Rising*. Thanks to editors Lucy Fowler, Ashley Richard, Anny Chen, and Jess Herdman.

'First-time smudge' was published in *ndn country*, the joint anthology by *cv2* and *Prairie Fire*. Thanks to editor Katherena Vermette.

'Blood quantum' and 'Please don't sue me, Meghan Trainor. This is not a pop song.' were published in *Canthius*. Thanks to editors Claire Farley and Cira Nickel.

'Junior Chicken' and 'Hey, spirit guides' were published in *talking about strawberries all of the time*. Thanks to editor Malcolm Curtis.

'Happy for a time' was published in *The Puritan*. Thanks to editor A. Light Zachary.

'At Christmas' was published in *Poetry is Dead*. Thanks to editor Kayla Czaga.

'I famously don't care' and 'How do you suffer?' were published in *Room*. Thanks to editor Nav Nagra.

'You're not allowed to die' and 'If you love it let it mould' were published in *Grain*. Thanks to editors Nicole Haldoupis and dee Hobsbawn-Smith.

Earlier versions of the following poems were originally published in the chapbook *I Don't Want to Tell You* with Rahila's Ghost Press

(2018): 'Puncture wounds,' 'Dear Dolphin,' 'Dear Dolphin II,' 'Are you there Molly? It's me, Hymen,' 'Home from A&W in winter after seven beers,' 'Exhibitionist,' 'Still fkn writing about him,' 'First-time smudge,' 'You,' and 'I go to the orthodontist.' Thanks to editor Selina Boan.

Thank you to the Coach House team — Susan Holbrook, Alana Wilcox, Crystal Sikma, and James Lindsay — for the labour, trust, and belief. So far, this is the coolest thing that's ever happened to me.

Thank you, Mali Fischer-Levine, for the cover art. She's perfect.

Thank you, Katherena Vermette, Amber Dawn, and Mallory Tater, for the generous blurbs, and for the bottomless pits of inspiration found in your books.

Thanks to my cohort at UBC who worked on many of these poems with me. An MFA is, indeed, many of the awful things people say it is, but it's also brimming with love and support.

Thank you, Ian Williams, for being this book's first eyes, for your play with language and ideas, and for the little confidence boosts. They kept me going.

Thank you, Catherine Hunter and Sheryda Warrener, for challenging me to reach beyond what I thought was my best. The 'you-can-do-better' teachers will always have my heart and gratitude.

Thank you to the team at Rahila's Ghost Press for your encouragement, resources, poetry, food, and friendship.

Thank you, Carter Selinger, for writing about the cat in the background of a porno and inspiring the title poem of this book.

Thank you to my partners in pandemic editing, Selina Boan, Sara DeWaal, and Hannah Green. Selina: We were in this together, baby! Thank you for the support, in writing and in life. You're a bright light. Sara: To be able to see inside your brain! Holy smokes are you ever brilliant. Thank you for your astute observations about the book and your kind encouragement. And Hannah: If anyone taught me what poetry can be and how to get there, it was you. Very grateful to learn from you, always. If the three of you are ever in the same room at the same time, I'm pretty sure it'll implode.

And more inspiring, supportive friends — Limarc Ambalina, Brandi Bird, Kate Black, Emma Cleary, Rebecca Cooke, Griffyn Crespeigne, Kristen Dubray, Taylor Follensbee, Keven Gauthier, Laura Ann Harris, Kennadi Herbert, Amy Higgins, Morgan Hill, Olga Holin, Jessica Johns, Ryan Kim, Tara McGuire, Kyle Nguyen, Tommy Partl, Issie Patterson, Cisca Rolleston Fuentes, Rachel Scramstad, Elena Sturk Lussier, Peter Takach, Jeremy Toon, Shristi Uprety, Briane Vance, and Ashtyn Walker — each of you is a little bit my soulmate.

To my grandparents, aunties, uncles, and cousins — there are so many of you and I love that for us! Thank you for being so nurturing and dysfunctional and gut-splittingly funny.

Dana Bridgeman Cross, Piper Cross, and Blaire Cross — your strength gives me strength.

To my pandemic pod, my family — Cara Nelissen, Jasmine Sealy, Ben Gardere, and Jules Ocean — thank you for being my people, for gassing me up and keeping me humble.

Thank you, B. Poetry may not have come to me if not for you. And neither would Ellie, who has taken such deep care of me all these years.

Vicki Blanchard, Curtis Blanchard, Abby Blanchard, and Reece · Blanchard. If there were words, which there aren't, they might be: Every day I go to sleep grateful, and that's your fault.

And thank you, truly, to whoever reads this book. All I've ever wanted to do was tell someone all my secrets. Thanks for listening.

ABOUT THE AUTHOR

Molly Cross-Blanchard is a white and Métis writer and editor born on Treaty 3 territory (Fort Frances, ON), raised on Treaty 6 territory (Prince Albert, SK), and living on the unceded territory of the Musqueam, Squamish, and Tsleil-Waututh peoples (Vancouver, BC). She holds an English BA from the University of Winnipeg and a Creative Writing MFA from the University of British Columbia, and is the publisher of *Room* magazine.

Typeset in Aragon and Amatic.

Printed at the Coach House on bpNichol Lane in Toronto, Ontario, on Zephyr Antique Laid paper, which was manufactured, acid-free, in Saint-Jérôme, Quebec, from second-growth forests. This book was printed with vegetable-based ink on a 1973 Heidelberg KORD offset litho press. Its pages were folded on a Baumfolder, gathered by hand, bound on a Sulby Auto-Minabinda, and trimmed on a Polar single-knife cutter.

Coach House is on the traditional territory of many nations including the Mississaugas of the Credit, the Anishnabeg, the Chippewa, the Haudenosaunee, and the Wendat peoples and is now home to many diverse First Nations, Inuit, and Métis peoples. We acknowledge that Toronto is covered by Treaty 13 with the Mississaugas of the Credit. We are grateful to live and work on this land.

Edited by Susan Holbrook
Designed by Crystal Sikma
Cover design by Crystal Sikma
Cover illustration by Mali Fischer-Levine, 2018

Coach House Books
80 bpNichol Lane
Toronto, ON M5S 3J4
Canada

416 979 2217
800 367 6360

mail@chbooks.com
www.chbooks.com